THE HISTORY OF THE ATLANTA FALCONS

THE HISTORY OF THE

ATLANTA

Published by Creative Education
123 South Broad Street
Mankato, Minnesota 56001
Creative Education is an imprint of The Creative Company.

DESIGN AND PRODUCTION BY **EVANSDAY DESIGN**

LIBRARY OF CONGRESS CATALOGING-IN-PUBLICATION DATA

Goodman, Michael E.
The history of the Atlanta Falcons / by Michael E. Goodman.
p. cm. — (NFL today)
Summary: Traces the history of the team from its beginnings through 2003.
ISBN 1-58341-287-5
1. Atlanta Falcons (Football team)—History—Juvenile literature.
[1. Atlanta Falcons (Football team)—History. 2. Football—History.]
I. Title. II. Series.

GV956.A85G665 2004
796.332'64'09758231—dc22   2003065035

First edition

9 8 7 6 5 4 3 2 1

COVER PHOTO: quarterback Michael Vick

PHOTOGRAPHS BY
AP/Wide World Photos, Corbis (Reuters, UPI/Corbis-Bettmann), Getty Images, SportsChrome USA

IN 1837, A RAILWAY CONNECTING POINT WAS ESTABLISHED IN NORTHWEST GEORGIA. AT FIRST, THE HUB WAS CALLED TERMINUS. THEN, IN 1842, RAILROAD EXECUTIVE AND FORMER GEORGIA GOVERNOR WILSON LUMP-KIN DECIDED TO RENAME IT IN HONOR OF HIS DAUGHTER. HER MIDDLE NAME WAS ATALANTA, WHICH HE SHORTENED TO ATLANTA. IT WASN'T LONG BEFORE THE CITY OF ATLANTA HAD GROWN INTO A LARGE METROPOLITAN CENTER.

IN JUNE 1965, THE NATIONAL FOOTBALL LEAGUE (NFL) CHOSE ATLANTA AS THE HOME FOR ITS FIRST FRANCHISE IN THE SOUTHEAST PART OF THE COUNTRY. SOON AFTER, TEAM OWNERS HELD A CONTEST TO NAME THE NEW CLUB. THE WIN-NING ENTRY CAME FROM A SCHOOLTEACHER, WHO SUGGESTED FALCONS BECAUSE "THE FALCON IS PROUD AND DIGNIFIED, WITH GREAT COURAGE AND FIGHT." AFTER TAKING THE FIELD FOR THE FIRST TIME, THE ATLANTA FALCONS WASTED NO TIME IN BUILDING A GREAT FOOTBALL TRADITION IN THE SOUTH.

[Running back William Andrews]

THE ATLANTA FALCONS began play in 1966 as the 15th team in the NFL. The club was loaded with mediocre veterans and youngsters and was led by a rookie coach named Norb Hecker. The Falcons didn't fly high in their first few years in the league, but they did feature a powerful defense led by hard-nosed linebacker Tommy Nobis, the Falcons' first-ever draft choice. The young star out of the University of Texas had a simple philosophy for playing defense. "I hit 'em right in the goozle—high and hard," he explained. "That way they don't go anywhere but down."

Unfortunately, Nobis couldn't play both defense and offense. Quarterback Randy Johnson, running back Junior Coffey, and receiver Alex Hawkins gave it their all, but the Falcons managed to score 20 or more points in a game only four times during the 1966 season. Atlanta finished its first year with a 3–11 record.

After the club went an embarrassing 1–12–1 its second year, the Falcons changed coaches and drafted another defensive star. The new coach was former NFL quarterback Norm Van Brocklin. The new defensive standout was end Claude Humphrey from Tennessee State University. Humphrey keyed a fierce Falcons pass rush and was named NFL Defensive Rookie of the Year in 1968.

By 1969, Van Brocklin's coaching system began to take effect, and the team's defense, led by Nobis, Humphrey, end John Zook, and cornerback Ken Reaves, battered opponents. The club finished 6–8, its best record yet. The Falcons continued to improve under Van Brocklin, recording their first winning season (7–6–1) in 1971. The defense was clicking on all cylinders, but the offense was still sputtering, and Van Brocklin's Falcons never became big winners.

LATE IN THE 1974 season, Van Brocklin was fired and replaced by defensive coordinator Marion Campbell. Campbell, who had built the Atlanta defense, had a new offensive weapon on hand in 1975: 6-foot-4 rookie quarterback Steve Bartkowski.

Falcons fans expected Bartkowski to turn the team around overnight. However, injuries and mistakes slowed his rise to stardom. He had trouble adjusting to pro defenses and suffered through a 4–10 rookie season. Then he missed much of the following two seasons with knee injuries. In 1978, Bartkowski returned healthy, but miserable preseason performances led new coach Leeman Bennett to bench the young quarterback. "That was the lowest I've ever been in my life," Bartkowski later recalled, "and it was also the best thing that ever happened to me."

Bartkowski gave up partying and became deeply religious. He regained the starting job by midseason in 1978 and—with the help of receivers Wallace Francis and Alfred Jenkins—led the team on a five-game winning streak. The Falcons finished 9–7 and made the playoffs for the first time in their history. After Atlanta beat the Philadelphia Eagles 14–13 in the playoffs, Falcons fans began dreaming of a Super Bowl. But the Dallas Cowboys gave them a rude awakening the next week, defeating the Falcons 27–20.

The Atlanta offense got a big boost the next season with the arrival of running back William Andrews. In college at Auburn University, Andrews was known more for his blocking than his rushing. At first, Coach Bennett planned to use Andrews mostly to block, but he ran so well in the preseason that Bennett decided to give him the ball.

Andrews made the coach look brilliant by setting a new team rushing record during the 1979 season with 1,023 yards. He achieved this success with a unique style: running slightly bent over with his head lowered. "I try to stay lower than my opponent," Andrews explained, "come at him in a ball, and then…POW!"

By 1980, the Falcons were ready for a run at a championship. That season, Andrews, Bartkowski, and Jenkins set new team records for rushing, passing, and pass receiving, respectively. The Falcons went 12–4 and won their first National Football Conference (NFC) Western Division title. In the playoffs, they faced off against the Dallas Cowboys in front of the largest crowd in Atlanta-Fulton County Stadium history. Atlanta led 27–17 in the fourth quarter, but Dallas rallied to hand the Falcons a crushing 30–27 defeat.

AFTER OPENING THE 1980s on a high note, the Falcons spent most of the rest of the decade near the bottom of the NFC standings. Atlanta fans enthusiastically cheered on one of the league's top offenses and then moaned as the club's weak defense allowed opponents to run up big scores.

The biggest cheers were for William Andrews, who seemed to get better and better. He made the Pro Bowl four straight years, from 1980 to 1983. Then a devastating knee injury put him on the sidelines for two seasons. He tried to make a comeback in 1986 but was soon forced to retire. Fortunately, while Andrews was out of the lineup, his backup, Gerald Riggs, emerged as a top runner. Riggs averaged nearly 1,000 yards per season between 1982 and 1988.

Another Atlanta favorite in the 1980s was lightning-quick wide receiver and kick returner Billy "White Shoes" Johnson. Johnson earned his nickname because of his bright footwear. Opponents hated watching those white shoes race by in a blur when Johnson returned punts and kickoffs for the Falcons.

Despite the great efforts of Riggs, Johnson, and Bartkowski, the Falcons went just 7–9 in 1983 and 4–12 in both 1984 and 1985. Even several coaching changes could not put Atlanta onto the winning track. Then, in the late 1980s, the team rebuilt around two key draft picks: quarterback Chris Miller from the University of Oregon and cornerback Deion Sanders from Florida State University.

The Falcons faced a challenge in signing Sanders, whose flashy moves as a cornerback and kick returner had earned him the nickname "Prime Time." The versatile athlete was also a top baseball player in the New York Yankees organization. Both franchises wanted Sanders's full-time services, but he had a different plan in mind. He figured he could play both sports—baseball in the summer and football in the fall.

Sanders put his plan into action in 1989. He played baseball most of the summer for the Yankees and then reported to Falcons training camp two days before the season opener. Even without much practice, Prime Time was electric in his first Falcons game, breaking tackles and outrunning opponents on a 68-yard punt return for a touchdown. Atlanta fans were delirious with excitement, and even coach Marion Campbell was impressed. "In my 27 years in the league, I've never experienced the buzz that goes through a stadium as when this guy gets near the football," he said.

THE FALCONS OPENED the 1990s with young stars such as Miller, Sanders, and wide receiver Andre Rison. They also had an eccentric new coach: Jerry Glanville. Glanville was brought in to shake things up in Atlanta, and he did. First, he changed the team's jerseys from red to black. Then he changed the club's attitude, installing a high-powered "Red Gun" passing offense developed by assistant coach June Jones and building an aggressive defense around linebacker Jesse Tuggle.

In 1991, Coach Glanville's Falcons went 10–6 and averaged more than 30 points per game in their victories. The club topped off the year by winning a playoff game for the first time in 13 years—a 27–20 road victory over the New Orleans Saints.

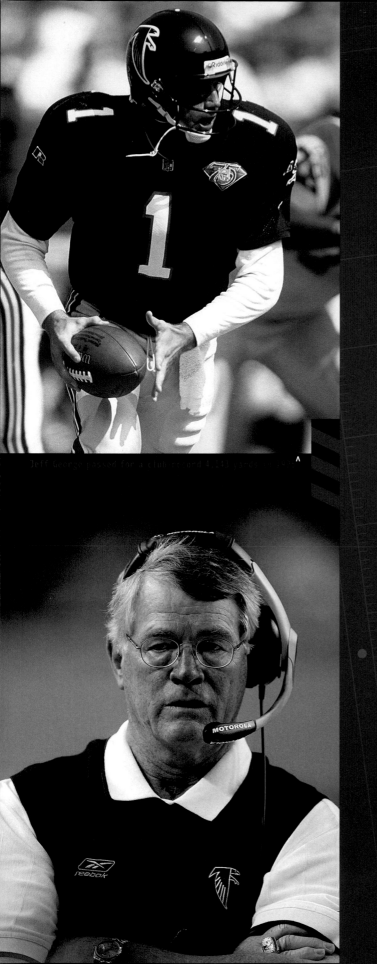

Jeff George passed for a club record 4,143 yards in 1995

The next season, the Falcons moved into a new home: Atlanta's giant Georgia Dome. Playing before record home crowds, the Falcons stumbled to two straight 6–10 seasons before Glanville was fired and replaced by June Jones. Coach Jones tried to design a new offense around the passing combination of quarterback Jeff George and wide receiver Terance Mathis, but he didn't have much luck.

Fortunately for Atlanta fans, positive change was coming. In January 1997, the Falcons replaced Jones with Dan Reeves, who had previously led the Denver Broncos to three Super Bowl appearances in the 1980s and had then built the New York Giants into winners. Reeves's hiring excited both Atlanta fans and players. "He's a winner," said Falcons defensive end Chuck Smith, "and he knows what it takes to get it done in this league."

ONE OF COACH REEVES'S first moves was to acquire

veteran quarterback Chris Chandler from the Houston

Oilers to provide much-needed experience and leader-

ship. Backed by running back Jamal Anderson and wide

receiver Bert Emanuel, Chandler soon got the offense run-

ning smoothly. The Falcons defense made an even more

remarkable turnaround. In 1997, Atlanta's defensive line

set a new club record with 55 quarterback sacks. Such

achievements left the Falcons brimming with confidence.

"It's time to stand up and be counted," announced cor-

nerback Ray Buchanan. "No more rebuilding and moral

victories. It's time to get it done."

Behind Anderson's strong running and Chandler's pinpoint passing, the 1998 Falcons offense pounded opposing defenses. Anderson set an NFL record with 410 carries and a club record with 1,846 rushing yards. He also created a touchdown dance to help fire up the team. After scoring, Anderson would hop from one foot to the other while flapping his arms like wings. Anderson's "Dirty Bird" dance helped inspire the Falcons to a 14–2 record and another NFC West title.

In the playoffs, Atlanta soared past San Francisco 20–18 to reach the NFC championship game against the 15–1 Minnesota Vikings. The two teams fought to a 27–27 tie in regulation and then kept battling into overtime. Atlanta's defense twice stopped the powerful Vikings offense before the Falcons won the game on a field goal by placekicker Morten Andersen. The once-lowly Falcons were Super Bowl bound at last!

In the Super Bowl against the defending champion Denver Broncos, the Falcons jumped out to a quick 3–0 lead. But the Atlanta defense could not hold down Denver quarterback John Elway, who directed a 34–19 Broncos win. "It's disappointing, but we lost to a fine team," said Chandler. "I guess our time is yet to come."

THE FALCONS FOLLOWED up their Super Bowl season with two disappointing years. Coach Reeves knew that the team needed a spark, so he engineered a trade with the San Diego Chargers to obtain the top pick in the 2001 NFL Draft. The Falcons then used it to select Michael Vick, a super-fast quarterback who had excelled as both a passer and runner during his college career at Virginia Tech University.

Vick replaced Chandler as the starting quarterback midway through his rookie season and then blossomed into one of the NFL's most exciting stars in 2002. Passing for nearly 3,000 yards and rushing for 777 more, Vick commanded a wide-open offense that propelled Atlanta back into the postseason. In round one of the playoffs, the high-flying Falcons handed the Green Bay Packers their first-ever playoff loss at Lambeau Field. Describing Vick's play, sportswriter Mike Holbrook noted, "He has shown

Peerless linebacker Keith Brooking joins Atlanta to lead ^

a penchant for doing the impossible and producing at least one play that leaves you saying, 'That's impossible,' or 'I've never seen that before.' He's the closest thing to a human highlight film as there is in the sport."

With Vick, running back T.J. Duckett, and receiver Peerless Price leading the offense, and with end Patrick Kerney and linebacker Keith Brooking spearheading the defense, the Falcons had football fans in the South flocking to the Georgia Dome in droves in 2003. "The huge crowds speak volumes about the enthusiasm this community is feeling about the Atlanta Falcons," said team vice president Dick Sullivan.

Although the Atlanta Falcons' history of nearly 40 years has had both ups and downs, it has never lacked excitement. Following in the footsteps of such Atlanta greats as Tommy Nobis, William Andrews, and Deion Sanders, today's Falcons plan to soon soar to the franchise's first Super Bowl trophy and make this hub of the South the center of the NFL.

INDEX >